LONDO

A wide river, a small village, a new country . . . 'We can make a town here,' said the Romans, and so Londinium began. Two thousand years later, that village is London, the biggest city in Britain, and millions of people visit it every year.

What brings them here? Some come to see the beautiful buildings and the great parades of Britain's royal family. Others like to walk along the River Thames, and through the green parks and gardens of this great city. And London is full of wonderful buildings, old and new, each with its own story.

People come in their thousands for the sport – to watch tennis at Wimbledon, football at Wembley, cricket at Lords, or to run in the London Marathon. Then there's shopping in Oxford Street, and the theatres of London's West End, and concerts – oh, there are hundreds of reasons to visit London.

Can't wait? Then come with us now, and get to know this wonderful city . . .

OXFORD BOOKWORMS LIBRARY
Factfiles

London
Stage 1 (400 headwords)

Factfiles Series Editor: Christine Lindop

JOHN ESCOTT

London

OXFORD UNIVERSITY PRESS

OXFORD
UNIVERSITY PRESS

Great Clarendon Street, Oxford OX2 6DP

Oxford University Press is a department of the University of Oxford.
It furthers the University's objective of excellence in research, scholarship,
and education by publishing worldwide in

Oxford New York

Auckland Cape Town Dar es Salaam Hong Kong Karachi
Kuala Lumpur Madrid Melbourne Mexico City Nairobi
New Delhi Shanghai Taipei Toronto

With offices in

Argentina Austria Brazil Chile Czech Republic France Greece
Guatemala Hungary Italy Japan Poland Portugal Singapore
South Korea Switzerland Thailand Turkey Ukraine Vietnam

OXFORD and OXFORD ENGLISH are registered trade marks of
Oxford University Press in the UK and in certain other countries

ISBN: 978 0 19 423374 3

A complete recording of this Bookworms edition of
London is available on audio CD. ISBN 978 0 19 423370 5

Printed in China

Word count (main text): 4810

For more information about the Oxford Bookworms Library,
visit www.oup.com/bookworms

The publishers would like to thank the following for permission to reproduce images:

Alamy pp 8 Jon Arnold Images, 36 (Ritz) Patrick Ward, 39 (bus) SC Photos, 44 (Buckingham Palace)
Alan Copson/Jon Arnold Images, (Kremlin) Jon Arnold/Jon Arnold Images; The Art Archive pp 2 Royal
Manuscript, View of London from the *Poems of Charles Duke of Orleans* (1394–1465)/British Museum/
Harper Collins, 5 India Section of the Dickinson's *Picture of the Great Exhibition*/Victoria and Albert
Museum/Eileen Tweedy; Axiom pp 34 Anna Watson, 35 Anthony Webb; Bridgeman Art Library
p 3 *The Great Fire of London* (September 1666) with Ludgate and Old St Paul's, c.1670 (oil on canvas)
by English School, (17th century)/© Yale Center for British Art, Paul Mellon Collection, USA;
Camera Press pp 11 (crown), 28 Richard Stonehouse; Collections p 26 Michael Jenner; Corbis pp 6
Murat Taner/Zefa, 7 (guards) Sveja-Foto/Zefa, 14 Nik Wheeler, 21 Bob Krist, 22 Tim Graham/Corbis
Sygma, 37 Adam Woolfitt; Empics pp 23 (zoo) Andrew Parsons/PA, 27 (statue) National Gallery/
Johnny Green/PA; Getty pp 15 Jason Hawkes, 16 Ann Cutting, 30 Peter Adams, 32 Odd Andersen/
AFP, 33 Carl de Souza/AFP, 38 Abid Katid, 40 Jason Hawkes; Imagestate pp 10 Benoit Pesle/Hoa-
Qui, 11 (Yeomen) Brian Lawrence, 13 Pictor, 19 Brian Lawrence; Lonely Planet Images pp 23 (canal)
Philip Game, 24 Rocco Fasano, 27 (Holmes) Neil Setchfield; Magnum Photos pp 20 Peter Marlow,
36 (chips) Peter Marlow, 50 Peter Marlow; David Noton p 7 (Windsor); Punchstock p 4 Allan Baxter;
PYMCA pp viii Giles Moberly, 31 NAKI; Rex Features pp 12 Paul Grover, 17 Alistair Muir, 25 Natural
History Museum, 39 (taxis) Ken Straiton; Superstock p 9 Johnny Stockshooter/AGEFotostock; View
p 18 Dennis Gilbert/architects Foster & Partners

This book is printed on paper from certified and well-managed sources.

CONTENTS

London today

1   A great city

Two thousand years ago, London was a small village by the River Thames. Then the Romans came and built a town, and thousands of people lived there. Now, in the twenty-first century, London is the biggest city in Britain, with more than seven million people. It is the capital city of the United Kingdom, the home of Queen Elizabeth the Second, and the home of the British government. Millions of visitors come to London every year.

The name 'London' comes from the Romans. People lived here before the Romans came, but we do not know very much about them. The Romans came to England in the year 43. Their ships came up the River Thames from the sea, and they built houses and other buildings next to the river. They built a bridge over the river, and they called the town Londinium. You can find out about London's early days, and about the Romans, at the Museum of London.

It was a rich town, and about 50,000 people lived in it. But soon after the year 400, the Romans left Londinium and went back to Rome, and for three hundred years London was a quiet place. Then people began to live in the town again, and it was soon rich and important. People called Angles, Saxons, and Jutes came to Britain from Germany, Holland, and Denmark. Then, in the ninth and tenth centuries, Danish ships came up the River Thames and destroyed many of Londinium's buildings.

In 1066, England had a new king – William the Conqueror from France. William came to live in London and built a castle there (today we know it as the Tower of London). London was now the biggest and most important city in England, and it got bigger and bigger. In 1509, when Henry the Eighth was king, there were 50,000 people in London. In 1600, when Henry's daughter Elizabeth the First was queen, there were 200,000 people.

William's castle – the Tower of London

The Great Fire of London in 1666

The plague often came to London, but 1665 was the worst year of all. In the hot summer that year thousands of people were ill, and 100,000 of them died. 1665 was called the Year of the Great Plague. Then a year later, in 1666, there was a big fire – the Great Fire of London. It began in a house in Pudding Lane, near London Bridge. Most houses were built of wood at that time, and fires love wood. The Great Fire of London went through street after street after street, and it did not stop for four days.

St Paul's Cathedral

More than a quarter of a million people lost their homes in the fire. It destroyed St Paul's Cathedral and eighty-eight other churches. But it also destroyed most of the worst old buildings. A new St Paul's Cathedral was built between 1675 and 1711.

In the eighteenth century, Britain was one of the most important countries in the world, and London was its most important city. Some Londoners were very rich, and they built some of the most beautiful houses in the city. Many of those houses are standing today. But at the same time, other people lived in cold, dark, wet houses.

Many of the buildings in London today were built when Queen Victoria was the queen. She was the queen for nearly sixty-four years, from 1837 when she was 18 years old, to 1901 when she died. In that time, many railways were built, and for the first time people could travel by train. Trains were much faster than coaches and horses, of course, and visitors came to London from all across the country. In 1851 there was the Great Exhibition at the Crystal Palace in Hyde Park. More than six million people came and saw the wonderful exhibits. In 1863, the world's first underground trains began to run in London, between Paddington and Farringdon. In 1881, there were more than three million people in the city.

In the twentieth century, German bombs destroyed many buildings in the Second World War (1939–1945). But they did not destroy St Paul's Cathedral. And now London has some of the world's most exciting new buildings.

Today, people from all over the world live in London, and you can hear about 300 different languages here. It is big, noisy, and often dirty – but people love to visit London.

The Great Exhibition at the Crystal Palace

2 Royal London

Visitors like to see the royal buildings, and sometimes you can go inside them too.

Buckingham Palace stands at the end of the Mall. The Mall is a long road, and it begins at Trafalgar Square. About 300 people work at the palace, because it is the Queen's home *and* her 'office'. Heads of governments and royal visitors from around the world meet the Queen here.

Buckingham Palace

At half-past eleven most mornings, the soldiers change the guard at Buckingham Palace. It takes about thirty minutes, and you can stand in front of the palace and watch. Hundreds of visitors do this every day.

In August and September you can usually visit some of the rooms in the palace, and see paintings by Vermeer, Rembrandt, and Rubens. You can also visit some of the palace gardens.

Soldiers changing the guard

The Queen's Gallery is in Buckingham Palace Road. Here you can see paintings from all over the world. Next to this is the Royal Mews, the home of the Queen's horses and coaches. You can visit the Queen's Gallery and the Royal Mews at most times of the year.

Some of the beautiful rooms of Kensington Palace in Kensington are also open to visitors.

Half an hour by train from the centre of London is Windsor Castle. You can visit the castle at any time of the year.

Windsor Castle

Hampton Court

Hampton Court stands next to the River Thames in a big park. This royal palace first opened to visitors at the time of Queen Victoria. You can take a train to Hampton Court from Waterloo Station. Or in the summer months, you can go there along the river from Westminster Pier.

Then there are the royal parades. On the second Saturday in June, London celebrates the Queen's birthday with a big parade – the Trooping of the Colour. It is not her real birthday – that is in April – but the weather is usually better in June. In the morning, she goes from Buckingham Palace to Horse Guards Parade in one of her coaches. Here soldiers carry the 'colour' (a big flag) past the Queen. Thousands of people stand in the Mall and watch the Queen and the soldiers go past.

The State Opening of Parliament usually happens in November, because in November the British government begins its work for the year. The Queen travels along the Mall to Westminster in a wonderful coach, and more than a hundred soldiers go along the Mall with her.

3 The City and the Tower of London

November is also the month of the Lord Mayor's Show. It happens on the second Saturday, and Londoners can see their new Lord Mayor. The Mayor travels from his home at Mansion House to the Strand in a 200-year-old coach.

The Lord Mayor is the most important person in London after the Queen. The first Mayor of London was Henry Fitzailwyn, in 1189. They were first called *Lord* Mayors in the time of King Henry the Eighth.

The City is the oldest part of London. It is the home of the Bank of England and many other big offices.

Old and new buildings in the City

Only about five thousand people live in the City, and at the weekends the streets are quiet. But between Monday and Friday, nearly half a million people go to work in the banks and offices there.

The Bank of England is more than three hundred years old. It is a very famous bank, and also has an interesting museum, with money from many different centuries.

The Tower of London is the City's oldest building. It stands by Tower Bridge, and next to the River Thames. In the past, it was a palace and a prison. Kings (and sometimes queens) put their most important prisoners there, and many of these prisoners never came out alive.

The Tower of London is not just one tower; it is eleven towers in different buildings. At the centre is the White Tower. This was built about 1078, and it was the tallest building in London at the time. You can see the Crown Jewels in the Jewel House, and visit the Bloody Tower.

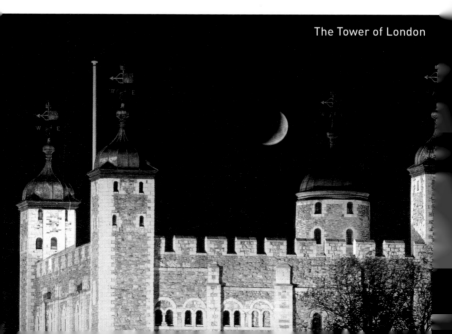

The Tower of London

The Crown Jewels

Yeoman Warders

In 1483, Edward the Fourth, the king of England, died. He had two young sons. So, was the next king Edward's older son? No, the next king was Edward's brother Richard, because Richard put Edward's two young sons in prison in the Tower. Nobody ever saw them again. Nearly 200 years later, people found bones in the Tower. Perhaps they were the bones of the king's dead sons – nobody knows.

Two other famous prisoners in the Tower were Anne Boleyn, wife of Henry the Eighth, and mother of Queen Elizabeth the First. Before she was queen, Elizabeth was also a prisoner in the Tower. Her sister, Queen Mary, put her there.

More than two million people visit the Tower every year. There are thirty-six Yeoman Warders, or Beefeaters, at the Tower. They tell visitors all about the Tower and its famous people.

Tower Bridge is more than 100 years old. It is one of London's most famous bridges. When tall ships go up the river, the centre of the bridge opens. You can learn more about the bridge at the exhibition there called the 'Tower Bridge Experience'.

The dome in St Paul's Cathedral

St Paul's Cathedral is in the centre of the City. Its dome is 110 metres high, and it is the second biggest dome in the world, after St Peter's in Rome.

The two bells in the tower are called Great Paul and Great Tom. Great Paul is the biggest bell in the United Kingdom. Great Tom rings every hour, and it also rings when a king or queen dies.

Also in the City is a building 60 metres high, called The Monument. It is near Pudding Lane, and was built because people wanted to remember the Great Fire of 1666.

4 Whitehall and Westminster

South of Trafalgar Square is a long road called Whitehall. Most of the buildings in this road are government offices.

There are two soldiers on horses outside Horse Guards Parade. Walk down the road to Parliament Square, and you go past Downing Street. It is not a long street. The Prime Minister – the head of the British Government – lives at 10 Downing Street.

In 1682, Sir George Downing built the street of houses near Whitehall Palace. There are only four houses here today, but they are very different now. King George the Second gave Number 10 to Sir Robert Walpole in 1735, and British Prime Ministers began to live in 10 Downing Street from that time.

Number 10
Downing Street

Westminster Abbey

After Whitehall comes Parliament Street and then Parliament Square, with its tall trees and its statue of Sir Winston Churchill. Churchill was Britain's Prime Minister at the time of the Second World War.

Next comes St Margaret's Street with Westminster Abbey and, across the street, the Houses of Parliament.

Westminster Abbey is London's oldest and perhaps most famous church. English kings and queens always have their coronations here – from the time of William the Conqueror in 1066 to today in the twenty-first century. Queen Elizabeth the Second had her coronation here in 1953. Thousands of people watched it in the Abbey, and millions more watched it on television – this was the first coronation on television.

The Houses of Parliament is the home of the British government. The clock high up on the building is called

The Houses of Parliament and Big Ben

Big Ben, but really Big Ben is the bell in the clock. You can hear Big Ben ring every hour. Four smaller bells ring on the quarter-hours.

In 1605 there was a man called Guy Fawkes. He and his friends did not like King James or his government, and they put a bomb under the Houses of Parliament. But nothing happened, because soldiers found Guy Fawkes and took him away. Now, British people celebrate this every year on 5 November with big fires and fireworks, and they often burn a figure of Guy Fawkes on the fire.

Guy Fawkes Night

5   By the river

You cannot see London without a visit to the River Thames. You can walk along the river, go across its many bridges, or go in a boat and see London from the river.

The first Globe Theatre was built at the time of Queen Elizabeth the First. People watched William Shakespeare's plays there. In 1997, a new Shakespeare's Globe Theatre opened, next to the River Thames. In the summer, you can visit the theatre and see Shakespeare's plays. Under the theatre is Shakespeare's Globe Exhibition. Here you can learn more about the work of England's most famous writer and the old and new Globe theatres.

The Globe Theatre

The Millennium Bridge and Tate Modern

Not far away is Tate Modern, an art gallery with 88 rooms of twentieth and twenty-first century art. The exhibitions change, so there is always something new. There are paintings by Matisse, Picasso, Jackson Pollock, Mark Rothko, Andy Warhol, and many more.

The Millennium Bridge is London's newest bridge – the first for 100 years. It goes across the river from outside Tate Modern. When it opened in the year 2000, hundreds of people walked across it – and it began to move under their feet! It was not open again for two years. People like walking across the bridge because there are good views of London and the river, and because there are no cars on the bridge.

Then there is the London Eye, a big wheel 135 metres high. It was built in 2000 and celebrates the Millennium. It never stops moving, but it moves very slowly. Visitors travel in the capsules on the wheel for 30 minutes, and when the weather is good, you can see for 40 kilometres across London. There are wonderful views of Buckingham Palace, the Houses of Parliament, and other famous buildings and parks in the city. Everybody loves going up in the London Eye.

The London Eye

Canary Wharf opened in 1991. It has three towers. The tower at One Canada Square is 240 metres high, and it is the tallest office building in Britain. You can go to Canary Wharf on the Docklands Light Railway, or take the

Jubilee Line train to Canary Wharf Station. You can also get there by boat. Visit the shops and restaurants, listen to music or watch theatre in the street, or visit the Museum in Docklands. In its twelve galleries you can learn about London's docks from the time of the Romans to now.

The Thames Barrier

There were bad floods in London in 1663 and 1928. Then, in 1953, more than 300 people died in a flood near the River Thames and in the east of England. So the Thames Barrier was built next to the Royal Victoria Dock. It opened in 1984, cost more than 400 million pounds, and is 520 metres long. When the sea is very high, the ten big gates on the barrier come up and stop the water. There is a visitor centre on the south side of the river, and you can see a video about the barrier there. The nearest train station is Charlton, but for the best view of the barrier take a boat from Greenwich.

6   Parks and gardens

When you are tired of buildings, you can visit one of London's many beautiful parks.

Hyde Park first opened to the people of London in the seventeenth century. It is not far from the shops of busy Oxford Street, but it is nice and quiet. You can walk or sit under the trees. In the centre is a lake called the Serpentine, and you can take a boat out on the water.

Boats on the Serpentine in Hyde Park

Diana, Princess of Wales playground

There are usually a lot of people at Speaker's Corner, near Marble Arch. Some people come here because they want to tell the world important or interesting things – about the government, or science, or the church, or the end of the world. They stand at the Corner, and call out to all the people around them. Other people stand and listen, and sometimes laugh too.

Kensington Gardens is next to Hyde Park. Here you can see a statue of Peter Pan, the famous boy in the book *Peter Pan* by J. M. Barrie. There is also a playground here, called the Diana, Princess of Wales playground. Many people want to remember Princess Diana. She lived near here in Kensington Palace, and the playground has lots of exciting things for children.

Regent's Park is the home of London Zoo. The zoo opened in 1828, and it has animals and birds from all over the world. There is also a theatre in the park. On a summer's evening, you can sit out and watch a play by

London Zoo

Shakespeare. Or you can see the park from the water – take a boat along the canal from Camden Lock to Little Venice. In the summer, you can listen to music in the park.

St James's Park is next to the Mall. It is a small park, but very beautiful, and it is the oldest of the royal parks. Lots of birds live on and around the lake in the centre of the park.

The canal in Regent's Park

7 More museums and galleries

The British Museum in Great Russell Street is the biggest museum in Britain, and the oldest museum in the world. It opened in 1759. There are 94 galleries (it is a four kilometre walk through all these galleries), a reading room, and bookshops. At the centre of the building is the beautiful Great Court.

The Great Court in the British Museum

The Museum of London at 150 London Wall opened in 1976. There you can learn about London and its people from its earliest times.

At the Natural History Museum in Cromwell Road you can learn all about our world and the people and animals in it. You can see the dinosaur exhibition – with moving dinosaurs – and many more beautiful and interesting things.

A dinosaur in the Natural History Museum

The Science Museum has more than 10,000 exhibits. Here you can learn about the science of the past, and the science of today. It also has an IMAX cinema.

A much smaller museum, at 48 Doughty Street, is the Dickens House Museum. The writer Charles Dickens lived in this house with his family for three years, from 1837 to 1839. He wrote two of his books here – *Oliver Twist* and *Nicholas Nickleby*. After Shakespeare, Dickens is England's next most famous writer.

Another important British writer, Sir Arthur Conan Doyle, wrote stories about Sherlock Holmes. The clever detective and his friend Dr Watson are now famous all over the world. The Sherlock Holmes Museum is at 221b Baker Street. The house was built in 1815, and in the stories Holmes lives at this address.

581

See → and be seen

HACKNEY
STATION

Harrods

TROLLEYBUS

EXV 253

The famous red
London bus at the
London Transport Museum

221b Baker Street   **The National Gallery**

Holmes did not really live in Baker Street, of course, but at the museum you can learn all about him. You can see Holmes's hat and Dr Watson's bedroom, and many things from the stories. And you can sit in Holmes's chair for a photograph.

The London Transport Museum is in Covent Garden, and tells the story of London's buses and underground trains from the early nineteenth century. There are lots of interesting things here; you can see films, 'drive' a London bus or underground train, and hear stories about buses in London during the Second World War.

Four million people visit the National Gallery in Trafalgar Square every year. There are more than 2,300 pictures here – the earliest from the thirteenth century.

Next to the National Gallery is the National Portrait Gallery, in St Martin's Place. Here you can see pictures of famous people. There are faces from the past – pictures of kings and queens, and of William Shakespeare – and faces from today – from Prince William to David Beckham.

Madame Tussauds

Tate Britain is at Millbank, past Lambeth Bridge. It is the home of British art, from the year 1500 to today. There are pictures by John Constable, J. M. W. Turner, and many other famous names in British art.

Madame Tussauds in Marylebone Road is famous for its wax figures. You can see famous people from the past and famous people of today – Abraham Lincoln, Mahatma Gandhi, Nelson Mandela, Beyoncé, and Brad Pitt. And in the 'Chamber of Horrors' you can see some very *bad* people.

The London Dungeon in Tooley Street is a 'Museum of Horror'. Half a million people visit it every year – but some do not stay very long!

Museums and art galleries can be very busy, but in the late afternoon it is often quieter. In many of the bigger museums and galleries, tickets are free.

8   Theatres, music, and sport

London's West End has some of the best theatres in the world, so tickets can be expensive. Sometimes they are fifty pounds or more. But you can get cheaper tickets too.

Go in the afternoon; tickets are often cheaper then. Or go to the *tkts* shop in Leicester Square. They have cheap tickets for many theatres in London, but the tickets are for that afternoon or evening. Or buy a ticket for 'the gods'. This is right at the top of the theatre, and it is always the cheapest place.

There is something for everybody – plays from hundreds of years ago, new plays by young writers, and of course *The Mousetrap*. This very English play by Agatha Christie began in 1952, and it is still going more than fifty years later. Thousands of visitors see it every year.

The National Theatre is in the South Bank Centre by the River Thames. It opened in 1976, and there are three different theatres in the building. There are also five restaurants and cafés, a big bookshop, free art exhibitions, and free music in the evenings.

At the Royal Opera House in Covent Garden you can hear wonderful music and singing from all over the world. For more music, go to the Royal Albert Hall in Kensington Gore next to Hyde Park.

Theatres in London's West End

But perhaps you want to see Madonna, or the Red Hot Chili Peppers, or Usher. Look at Earls Court, Wembley Stadium, and the Brixton Academy. And the place for cinemas is Leicester Square. You can see dozens of different films here, and when there is a premiere, you can see the stars with their beautiful clothes and expensive cars.

The Barbican Arts Centre is at Silk Street. It has three cinemas, two theatres, a concert hall, and one of London's biggest art galleries. There is also a school of music and a library. The nearest underground station is Barbican.

Then there are London's clubs – hundreds of them. There are small clubs, big clubs, clubs with 70s music, clubs with the latest music. Fabric, Ministry of Sound, and Po Na Na are all famous clubs, but there are lots of new ones too. Many clubs are open till 2 a.m. or later. In many clubs tickets are more expensive late at night, so go early. There are lots of clubs in Soho and Covent Garden, and also in Notting Hill, York Way, and Clerkenwell.

Dancing at a London club

A game of cricket

Cricket is a very English game. You can see it at Lord's Cricket Ground in St John's Wood in North London or the Oval near Vauxhall in South London.

London is the home of some of the most famous names in English football. Chelsea play at Stamford Bridge, Fulham Road, SW6, and Tottenham Hotspur play at White Hart Lane, High Road, N17.

The world's best tennis players come to London every June for the Wimbledon Lawn Tennis Championships. You can see them at the All England Lawn Tennis Club in Church Road, Wimbledon, but you need to go early. Sometimes people wait all night for tickets!

The Oxford and Cambridge University Boat Race began in Henley-on-Thames in 1829. These days the race, nearly 7 kilometres long, begins in Putney and ends in Mortlake. It is in March or April every year. About 250,000 people stand beside the river or on the bridges and watch the two fast boats.

The London Marathon happens on a Sunday in April. The runners start at Greenwich and run through the streets of London to Westminster. Some of the world's best runners come to London for the race – and thousands of other people run for three, four, five or more hours to finish the marathon. Today more than half a million people can say, 'I finished the London Marathon.'

In 1908 and 1948 people came to London from all over the world for the Olympic Games. Now the Olympic Games are coming to London for the third time in 2012. Many Londoners are excited about this.

The London Marathon

9 Shopping and eating

The Harrods bag

You can buy nearly anything in London. Many of the most famous (and expensive) shops are in Regent Street, Bond Street, and in Knightsbridge. The most famous shop in all of the city – some people say the most famous in the world – is Harrods, in Knightsbridge. It began in 1849 when Henry Charles Harrod opened a small food shop in Brompton Road. The building in Knightsbridge opened in 1905, and now 4,000 people work there. Some people go there and buy something very, very small, just because they want the bag with the famous 'Harrods' name on it.

Oxford Street has many big shops – Selfridges, Marks and Spencer, Debenhams. For smaller shops, go to Covent Garden. Charing Cross Road is famous for its bookshops. There are lots of them, and they sell old and new books.

At weekends you can visit some of London's markets. Petticoat Lane market (open on Sundays) is in Middlesex Street, and has cheap clothes and things for the home. At the market in Portobello Road (open on Saturdays) you

A London market

Fish and chips

can buy old clocks, old chairs and tables, and hundreds of other things. At Brick Lane market (open on Sundays) in the East End, you can buy nearly everything. Old Spitalfields Market in Commercial Street (open on Sundays) has some of the latest clothes in town – and they're cheap!

When it is time for food, London has everything. You can have dinner in an expensive restaurant for hundreds of pounds – or you can buy a sandwich for not very much at all. You can eat in cafés or bars, you can buy food and take it away, and of course you can buy English fish and chips!

London has restaurants from nearly every country in the world, and not all of

Afternoon tea at the Ritz

them are expensive. You can find food from Italy, Mexico, Spain, India, China, Russia, and many other countries. There are hundreds of good restaurants in Piccadilly, Soho, Leicester Square, and Covent Garden, and more in Kensingston, Knightsbridge, and Chelsea.

For a very English afternoon, go to the Ritz in Piccadilly or the Savoy Hotel in the Strand for afternoon tea. You can listen to music, drink tea, and eat wonderful food. But remember to take a lot of money with you!

And do not forget about pubs. There are thousands of pubs in London. In many pubs you can eat and drink, and pub food is often cheap and good.

A London pub

10 Travelling

When you come to London, do not bring a car. Take an underground train or a bus. Or walk!

The Underground – also called the Tube – is fast. The trains go from about 5 a.m. (later at weekends) to about midnight. Buy your ticket before you get on the train, and don't lose it. You need it when you begin your journey and when you finish it.

Between eight o'clock and ten o'clock in the morning, and between four o'clock and six o'clock in the evening, thousands of people are going to and from work. This is the morning and evening 'rush hour', and you cannot

The London Underground

You can see much more from a bus

move easily on the trains and the buses. It is much nicer and quieter when you do not travel in the rush hour.

You can see much more of London from the famous red buses than from the Tube. There are buses for visitors too; they take you around many of the interesting places in the city. It takes about one and a half hours, but you can get off the bus for a visit and get on again later.

Or you can travel in one of London's famous black taxis (also called 'black cabs'). Most of them are black but some are blue, red, green, or white. Drivers must know all the 25,000 streets in the centre of London before they can drive a taxi here.

Black cabs

Why not go by boat along the River Thames? Boats leave Westminster Pier, Waterloo Pier, and Embankment Pier, and they go to Tower Pier, Greenwich, and (between April and October) Hampton Court.

Big red buses . . . Buckingham Palace . . . the London Eye . . . Big Ben – these are only some of the things in London. It is a big, beautiful, noisy, and exciting city. More than eleven million visitors come every year from countries all over the world.

So, when are you coming to London?

GLOSSARY

art pictures and other beautiful things that people like to look at

bank a building or business for keeping money safely

bar a room where people can buy and have drinks

bell a metal thing that makes a sound when something touches it

boat a small ship for travelling on water

bomb a thing that explodes and damages people or things

bone one of the hard white parts inside an animal's or a person's body

bridge something built high to go over a river or road

café a place where people can buy and eat food and drink

capital (**city**) the most important city in a country

celebrate to enjoy yourself because you have a special reason to be happy

century a time of 100 years

church a building where people pray to God

clothes things you wear, e.g. shirts, trousers, dresses

club a place where you go to dance and listen to music

coach a vehicle with four wheels that is pulled by horses

concert music played for a lot of people

coronation the special day when a man is made king, or a woman is made queen

destroy when something is destroyed, it is dead and finished (e.g. fire destroys a forest)

docks a place on a river or by the sea where ships bring people and things

exhibit *(n)* something people go to look at e.g. in a museum or gallery

figure something made to look like the head and body of a person

flag a piece of cloth with a special pattern on it; every country has a flag

flood when there is a flood, a lot of water covers the land

food   what you eat

gallery   a place where you can see paintings and other kinds of art

government   a group of people who control a country

horror   very great fear

horse   a big animal that can carry people and pull heavy things

king   the most important man in a country

museum   a place where you can look at old or interesting things

music   when you sing or play an instrument, you make music

Olympic Games   games held every four years for sports people from many different countries

painting   a picture made with paint

parade   a line of people who are walking together for a special reason, while other people watch them

plague   a very bad illness that makes thousands of people die

play *(n)*   you go to the theatre to see a play

prison   a building for bad people; they stay there and cannot leave

queen   the most important woman in a country

restaurant   a place where people can buy and eat meals

ring *(v)*   to make a sound like a bell

royal   of or about a king or queen

science   the study of natural things

St   short for 'Saint', part of the name of a very good or holy person

statue   the shape of a person or an animal that is made of stone or metal

top   the highest part of something

view   what you can see from a certain place

war   fighting between countries or groups of people

wax   the soft stuff that candles are made from

London

ACTIVITIES

ACTIVITIES

Before Reading

1 Here are six famous places. Can you match the names
with the photos?

*The White House / the Kremlin / Buckingham Palace / the
Eiffel Tower / the Houses of Parliament / the Parthenon*

2 How many of these places are you going to find in a
book about London? Which places are they? What do
you know about them? What other places can you name
in London, and what do you know about them?

ACTIVITIES

While Reading

Read Chapter 1, then put these sentences in the right order.

1 The Great Fire of London destroyed a lot of buildings.
2 William the Conqueror built a castle in London.
3 Thousands of people died in the Great Plague.
4 The world's first underground trains began to run.
5 New Saint Paul's Cathedral was built.
6 The Romans came to London.
7 People came to see the Great Exhibition.
8 Elizabeth the First was queen.
9 Bombs destroyed many of London's buildings during the Second World War.
10 Danish ships came and destroyed many buildings.

Read Chapter 2. Are these sentences true (T) or false (F)? Change the false sentences into true ones.

1 About 300 people work in Buckingham Palace.
2 When you visit the Royal Mews you can see the Queen's paintings.
3 You can visit Windsor Castle all year round.
4 Hampton Court is on the River Thames.
5 The big parade called the Trooping of the Colour is on the Queen's birthday in April.
6 When the Queen goes to open Parliament, she rides a beautiful white horse.

Read Chapter 3, then circle the correct words in each sentence.

1 The City is *busy / quiet* during the week.
2 The Tower of London is the *oldest / tallest* building in the City.
3 Queen Elizabeth the First was once a *prisoner / warder* in the Tower of London.
4 The dome of St Paul's Cathedral is the biggest in *Britain / the world*.
5 Great *Paul / Tom* rings when a king dies.
6 At the Monument people remember the year of the Great *Plague / Fire*.

Read Chapters 4 and 5. Choose the best question word for these sentences, and then answer them.

Who / What / Why
1 . . . lives at 10 Downing Street?
2 . . . can you see in Parliament Square?
3 . . . was different about the coronation in 1953?
4 . . . is Big Ben?
5 . . . do people do every year to remember Guy Fawkes?
6 . . . wrote plays for the first Globe Theatre?
7 . . . can you see in Tate Modern?
8 . . . do people like to go on the Millennium Bridge?
9 . . . can you do at the London Eye?
10 . . . is the tallest office building in Britain?
11 . . . happens at the Thames Barrier when the sea is very high?

Read Chapters 6 and 7. Then complete these sentences with the names of places.

1 In _____ you can take a boat out on the Serpentine.

2 People remember Diana, Princess of Wales, at the playground in _____ .

3 You can see animals from all over the world at the zoo in _____ .

4 The bones of the world's biggest animal are in the _____ .

5 In the Sherlock Holmes stories the famous detective lives at _____ .

6 The _____ is full of pictures of famous people.

7 _____ has paintings by Constable and Turner.

8 Half a million people visit the _____ every year.

Read Chapters 8, 9, and 10, and answer these questions.

1 How long ago did *The Mousetrap* begin in London?

2 Why do people go to Fabric and Ministry of Sound?

3 What can you see at the Oval?

4 Where does the London Marathon end?

5 What is the most famous shop in London?

6 Where is a good place to look for books?

7 Which markets have cheap clothes?

8 What do people enjoy at the Ritz in the afternoon?

9 What colour are London's famous buses?

10 How many streets do taxi drivers need to know?

ACTIVITIES

After Reading

1 Here is an e-mail about a visit to London. Circle the correct words.

From: Alice
Subject: London

Hello/Goodbye from London!

I *arrived/left* here on Thursday. What a wonderful *town/city*! On *Saturday/Sunday* we saw the *Trooping of the Colour/Lord Mayor's Show*. It's a big *exhibition/parade* for the *King's/Queen's* birthday. We saw her go past in a beautiful *coach/car*.

On Monday we went to the River *Thames/Tyne*. We walked across *the Millennium Bridge/Tower Bridge* to *the National Gallery/Tate Modern* and went to look at the *films/paintings*. Then we had a *ride/walk* in the *Thames Barrier/London Eye*. The weather was *good/bad*, so we could see *Hyde/Central* Park, Saint *Patrick's/Paul's* Cathedral, and a lot of other places.

Now it's time for some shopping. Tomorrow I'm going to *the City/Knightsbridge*, because I want to visit Harrods. After that I'm going to the *Brixton Academy/Ritz* to have *afternoon tea/fish and chips* – it's a very *English/British* thing to do!

See you soon

Alice

2 Find these words in the word search below, and draw
  lines through them. The words go from left to right, and
  from top to bottom.

art, bar, capital, century, church, club, concert, coronation,
destroy, docks, flood, food, gallery, government, king,
museum, music, painting, prison, royal, view

G	O	V	E	R	N	M	E	N	T	K	S
H	F	C	C	A	P	I	T	A	L	I	A
K	O	O	B	A	R	E	S	V	P	N	C
M	O	R	P	A	I	N	T	I	N	G	O
U	D	O	C	K	S	A	C	E	R	G	N
S	E	N	A	R	O	R	H	W	O	A	C
E	E	A	C	E	N	T	U	R	Y	L	E
U	S	T	C	L	U	B	R	G	A	L	R
M	L	I	M	U	S	I	C	O	L	E	T
F	L	O	O	D	B	E	H	T	H	R	E
A	T	N	R	D	E	S	T	R	O	Y	E

Now write down all the letters that do not have lines
through them, beginning with the first line and going
across each line to the end. You now have 24 letters,
which make the name of a place.

1 What is the name, and where is this place?
2 What can you see there?
3 When did it open?

3 Here is a new photo for the book. Find the best place in
  the book to put the picture, and answer these questions.

  The picture goes on page ___.
  1 Where was the photographer?
  2 Would you like to go there?
  3 What can you see in the photo?

Now write a caption for the photo.

Caption: _____

4 **It is the year 2100. What is London like? Tick the sentences you agree with.**

	Yes	No
1 Everybody speaks English.	☐	☐
2 Nobody lives near the river because of the floods.	☐	☐
3 There are no cars in the centre of London.	☐	☐
4 Buckingham Palace is now a hotel.	☐	☐
5 Fish is very expensive, so only rich people eat fish and chips.	☐	☐

Now write two sentences of your own.

5 **Would you like to visit London? Why / Why not? What five things would you like to see and do in London? What would you like to see first? What is the most interesting thing about the city for you?**

6 **Compare London and your city or town. You can use the information in this book. These websites can help you too: www.visitlondon.com, www.visitbritain.com, www.enjoyengland.com**

You can begin like this:

There are 7 million people in London, but in (my city) there are _____ . In London, people speak English and about 300 more languages; in (my city) they speak . . .

ABOUT THE AUTHOR

John Escott worked in business before becoming a writer. Since then he has written many books for readers of all ages. He was born in Somerset, in the west of England, but now lives in Bournemouth on the south coast. When he is not working, he likes looking for long-forgotten books in small backstreet bookshops, watching old Hollywood films on video, and walking for miles along empty beaches. He also enjoys visiting London and going to the art galleries and museums.

John has written or retold many stories for both Oxford Dominoes and Oxford Bookworms. His other Factfiles titles are *New York* and *England* (both at Stage 1) and *Great Crimes* (at Stage 4).

OXFORD BOOKWORMS LIBRARY

Classics • Crime & Mystery • Factfiles • Fantasy & Horror
Human Interest • Playscripts • Thriller & Adventure
True Stories • World Stories

The OXFORD BOOKWORMS LIBRARY provides enjoyable reading in English, with a wide range of classic and modern fiction, non-fiction, and plays. It includes original and adapted texts in seven carefully graded language stages, which take learners from beginner to advanced level. An overview is given on the next pages.

All Stage 1 titles are available as audio recordings, as well as over eighty other titles from Starter to Stage 6. All Starters and many titles at Stages 1 to 4 are specially recommended for younger learners. Every Bookworm is illustrated, and Starters and Factfiles have full-colour illustrations.

The OXFORD BOOKWORMS LIBRARY also offers extensive support. Each book contains an introduction to the story, notes about the author, a glossary, and activities. Additional resources include tests and worksheets, and answers for these and for the activities in the books. There is advice on running a class library, using audio recordings, and the many ways of using Oxford Bookworms in reading programmes. Resource materials are available on the website <www.oup.com/bookworms>.

The *Oxford Bookworms Collection* is a series for advanced learners. It consists of volumes of short stories by well-known authors, both classic and modern. Texts are not abridged or adapted in any way, but carefully selected to be accessible to the advanced student.

You can find details and a full list of titles in the *Oxford Bookworms Library Catalogue* and *Oxford English Language Teaching Catalogues*, and on the website <www.oup.com/bookworms>.

THE OXFORD BOOKWORMS LIBRARY
GRADING AND SAMPLE EXTRACTS

STARTER • 250 HEADWORDS

present simple – present continuous – imperative –
can/cannot, must – *going to* (future) – simple gerunds …

Her phone is ringing – but where is it?

Sally gets out of bed and looks in her bag. No phone.
She looks under the bed. No phone. Then she looks behind
the door. There is her phone. Sally picks up her phone and
answers it. ***Sally's Phone***

STAGE 1 • 400 HEADWORDS

… past simple – coordination with *and, but, or* –
subordination with *before, after, when, because, so* …

I knew him in Persia. He was a famous builder and I
worked with him there. For a time I was his friend, but
not for long. When he came to Paris, I came after him –
I wanted to watch him. He was a very clever, very dangerous
man. ***The Phantom of the Opera***

STAGE 2 • 700 HEADWORDS

… present perfect – *will* (future) – *(don't) have to, must not, could* –
comparison of adjectives – simple *if* clauses – past continuous –
tag questions – *ask/tell* + infinitive …

While I was writing these words in my diary, I decided
what to do. I must try to escape. I shall try to get down the
wall outside. The window is high above the ground, but
I have to try. I shall take some of the gold with me – if I
escape, perhaps it will be helpful later. ***Dracula***

STAGE 3 • 1000 HEADWORDS

… should, may – present perfect continuous – *used to* – past perfect
– causative – relative clauses – indirect statements …

Of course, it was most important that no one should see
Colin, Mary, or Dickon entering the secret garden. So Colin
gave orders to the gardeners that they must all keep away
from that part of the garden in future. *The Secret Garden*

STAGE 4 • 1400 HEADWORDS

… past perfect continuous – passive (simple forms) –
would conditional clauses – indirect questions –
relatives with *where/when* – gerunds after prepositions/phrases …

I was glad. Now Hyde could not show his face to the world
again. If he did, every honest man in London would be proud
to report him to the police. *Dr Jekyll and Mr Hyde*

STAGE 5 • 1800 HEADWORDS

… future continuous – future perfect –
passive (modals, continuous forms) –
would have conditional clauses – modals + perfect infinitive …

If he had spoken Estella's name, I would have hit him. I was so
angry with him, and so depressed about my future, that I could
not eat the breakfast. Instead I went straight to the old house.
Great Expectations

STAGE 6 • 2500 HEADWORDS

… passive (infinitives, gerunds) – advanced modal meanings –
clauses of concession, condition

When I stepped up to the piano, I was confident. It was as if I
knew that the prodigy side of me really did exist. And when I
started to play, I was so caught up in how lovely I looked that
I didn't worry how I would sound. *The Joy Luck Club*

BOOKWORMS · FACTFILES · STAGE 1

England

JOHN ESCOTT

Twenty-five million people come to England every year, and some never go out of London. But England too is full of interesting places to visit and things to do. There are big noisy cities with great shops and theatres, and quiet little villages. You can visit old castles and beautiful churches – or go to festivals with music twenty-four hours a day. You can have an English afternoon tea, walk on long white beaches, watch a great game of football, or visit a country house. Yes, England has something for everybody – what has it got for you?

BOOKWORMS · FACTFILES · STAGE 1

New York

JOHN ESCOTT

What can you do in New York? Everything! You can go to some of the world's most famous shops, watch a baseball game, go to the top of a skyscraper, see a concert in Central Park, eat a sandwich in a New York deli, see a show in a Broadway theatre.

New York is big, noisy, and exciting, and it's waiting for you. Open the book and come with us to this wonderful city.